A Level Notes

Ian McEwan's Enduring Love

Jane Gibson

Cotton & Jarrett

First published in the UK in 2003 by:

Cotton & Jarrett
Ash Tree House
20 Scalford Road
Eastwell
Leicestershire
LE14 2EJ

ISBN-13   978-0954652005
ISBN-10   0-9546520-0-2

Third printing 2008

Contents

Preface

Ian McEwan's novel Enduring Love delighted me as a reader, and challenged me as a person to recognise the inaccuracy and bias in my own perception and modeling of reality. It is a book that richly repays study and which has been rewarding to teach at Advanced Level. I have gained a great deal from the insights of my students as well as those of my friends and partner Dave.

In order to achieve a top grade at A-level it is necessary to have a deep and individual understanding of the novel. Markers soon become aware of which particular set of notes a candidate has read and is now regurgitating as his or her own. I have attempted to point out what I believe to be the great and profound themes of this well-crafted novel, but my aim has been to get the students to think for themselves and to þnd their own reading of the novel. To this end most of my comments on the novel take the form of an observation followed by a question. This is also an excellent way of studying the novel as a class. Asking a question demands an answer of the mind, and it is in þnding the right questions that the required level of individual understanding is gained.

The þnal three sections of this booklet are sample essays, closely based on ones handed in by my A-level class. These show the quality of analysis and individual reading which is necessary for an A grade.

Introduction

Enduring Love can best be summed up as a psychological thriller, which engages with contemporary challenging ideas. These ideas have exercised philosophical thought throughout the 20th century to the present day. Ian McEwan carefully crafts his novel to combine excitement and originality with a challenge to the reader to examine the beliefs that he or she may hold about every aspect of life, the society we live in, and the truths that we hold about the human condition; that is, what it means to be a person living in a given society at a particular time in history. The behavioural scientist B. F. Skinner claimed, "we live in a scientiÞc age," and by this he meant that not only are we guided by science, but that we have, to some extent, created a new scale of values and ideals based upon scientiÞc research. This new system is not value free; rather it has been seen as a moral signpost, which could take the place of religion. Science has developed over the last century to the extent that the physical sciences have been idealised and treated as though they are the only possible forms for rational thought across the whole range of knowledge. Science, Art and Religion are represented in this novel by the central protagonists. All three have strong opinions and claim to answer the question, 'what can we know for sure?' The ßawed way in which beliefs are constructed by every character sets the context for the novel, and is the author's challenge to us to question our own construing of reality.

McEwan examines ideas which challenge the concept that science offers absolutes of understanding, and the linked belief in the inevitability of progress and the omnicompetence of Science. In chapter nineteen we are introduced to Clarissa's Godfather, a scientist who speaks of past eminences in the Þeld of science who, "couldn't, or wouldn't" see the truth of the scientiÞc evidence before them because the evidence conßicted with their 'pet theories'. The facts may have been inviolable, but the interpretation of the facts was skewed because an individual's viewpoint makes a great difference to how we see things. We all see selectively. The character Jean Logan illustrates this effectively.

All perception takes in only a fraction of what is given to it, and all thought narrows that fraction still further in trying to make sense of it. Jean Logan asserts that she knows what killed her husband. As Joe says, "believing is seeing." This means that what we see is real enough, but it is always partial, and a good deal of the narrowing is within our own control. As it says in the Talmud, "We see things not as they are, rather as we are."

It is interesting that Clarissa Mellon is an academic whose specialist subject is the Romantic poet John Keats. Clarissa attempts, (as do all biographers) to know the subject of their research by examining letters and witness accounts as well as the life work of their subject, to establish the truth about a life and a character. This truth will of course always be a collage of perception: a subjective presentation of certain facts; possibly other facts will be omitted because they are inconsistent with an idea in the mind of the biographer.

Clarissa is of course the great love in the life of the central protagonist and narrator Joe Rose. The important point is that for Keats, the imaginative mind was diametrically opposed to the intellect; "It was capable of being in uncertainties, mysteries, doubts, without any irritable reaching after fact and reason." He calls this negative capability. Clarissa says to Joe on page 33, "You're such a dope. You're so rational sometimes you're like a child." This leads Joe to ponder, "Did she mean that rationality was a kind of innocence?"

As Joe grapples with the meaning of Parry's irrational obsession and his enduring love for him, rational explanations, indeed science, cannot answer the question that is posed in the novel: Why do human beings fall in love? If being in love is the spark that Þres the engine of procreation (as evolutionary psychologists believe), then what is the evolutionary investment of Jed's love for Joe? Why do some people become prey to psychotic delusion, and what do we mean by psychological normality? As all the characters in the novel are at some time or other given to delusions, is madness just a matter of degree? Joe's scientiÞc reasoning is often seen as an over-simpliÞcation and therefore reductive by Clarissa. On page 70 Clarissa takes issue with Joe's stance on evolutionary psychology; that is the belief that behaviour is determined by our genetic impetus for survival. This is the thesis of Richard Dawkins in his highly acclaimed book, 'The SelÞsh Gene', and it is important because it is clear that scientiÞc thinking provides the contextual backdrop for the ideas in this novel. Clarissa calls these ideas, "the new fundamentalism" and asserts that it is, "rationalism gone berserk." Like Keats, Clarissa believes that, "Science strips everything down and in the process some larger meaning is lost."

This novel takes as its central themes Love, Science, Knowledge (what we can know for sure and what must remain uncertain) and

Perception. In chapter three Clarissa jokingly tells Joe, "the rationalist cracks at last," and throughout the novel, which opens with the sentence, "The beginning is simple to mark," we see Joe grapple with ideas which will not conform to simple, rational explanation. At the end of the novel Joe says: "In a world in which logic was the engine of feeling... we should have set about rebuilding our lives, but such logic would have been inhuman." Joe realises that feelings are often irrational; that we all have feelings and our interpretation facts is not exempted from our feelings. To this extent scientiþc data that is interpreted subjectively cannot be infallible, in this novel all knowledge is presented as insecure and suspect. Science has from the outset in Enlightenment thinking been associated with two ambitious claims, infallibility, and the formal unity of thought sought by Descartes, who attempted in his famous quest for a rational system based upon a single unassailable certainty. His aim was to þnd a single þrm truth from which all others could be seen to follow. Yet as Joe discovered, our humanity means that we cannot demand infallibility, and that rationality does not require us to be infallible. Even our short-term memory as shown in the ice cream incident is fallible. The police inspector's point was that the unreliability of recollection made truth a very slippery commodity, the balloon on the cover of the novel is an eye; an eye which sees the truth of the real world because it is poised above it, "seeing the multiplicity and variety of matter in the universe." It is the objective point to view the many and various points of view presented in this engaging and challenging novel.

Chapter 1

The Truth is seldom pure, and never simple

• The novel commences with the statement, "The beginning is simple to mark." Consider how this sentence creates an effective hook for the rest of the story.

• McEwan lists facts about the picnic: "data that he can be sure of." This narrative is written in retrospect; why do you think that unassailable facts are important?

• Consider the choice of language for its effectiveness as a hook for the reader, and also its hints about the central themes of the novel: "What idiocy... Labyrinths... Sprinting away from our happiness ..."

• The narrator, Joe Rose writes, "I see us from three hundred feet up. ... the knowable perspective." This is the buzzard's perspective on the events. What point is Joe trying to make?

• Remember that Joe is a scientist. What words can you see from the semantic Þeld of science that shows that his narrative is coloured by his profession?

• Joe uses the expression "mathematical grace." Maths is the truth we can share, the truth we can know. He also writes of ourselves and all our thoughts. What sense do you make of the juxtaposition of ideas?

• We are introduced to Clarissa and told that she is researching the Romantic poet John Keats. Clarissa is searching for a last letter to Keat's mistress Fanny Brawne because she is certain that, "love that did not Þnd its expression in a letter was not perfect." What do you understand to be the relevance of this information in the development of your understanding of (a) Clarissa's character, and (b) the theme of knowledge and perception that is already emerging in the novel? Joe says in answer to Clarissa's vehemence, "All that sincerity would permit me were the facts." What insight does this provide that these two lovers have a fundamentally different perspective on life?

• Joe analyses the accident and his own part in the rescue attempt. He says: "I know that if I had been the uncontested leader... Later I heard some of the others say the same thing about themselves." Similarly none of the men believe that they were the Þrst to let go. Could these beliefs have all been consistent?

• Examine the ways in which McEwan uses language to heighten the drama and tension of the rescue attempt (p.13).

• Note the painstaking examination of the facts known to Joe, using language like; "another variable was added to the equation." Mixed with objective facts are subjective value judgments, "What is certain is that if we had not broken ranks... It was every man for himself."

• Joe tries to formulate a moral code based upon logical thought, "we are good when it makes sense, a good society is one that makes sense of being good..." (p.15)

• Joe's choice of language on the Þnal page of the chapter, when describing the natural phenomena that contributed to the accident is interesting: "furious thermal... freak physical law... ruthless gravity..."

Chapter 2

The shock of a fatal accident

- We are introduced to Jed Parry following the accident. The shock of witnessing a violent death is analysed in detail.

- Joe's painstaking need to establish facts and create a firm foundation for excavating the truth is reflected in his use of mathematical language.

- McEwan hints at the importance of events subsequent to the accident: "The afternoon could have ended in mere tragedy" (p.18).

- Dramatic impact is created by comparing Logan's fall to earth to a recurrent nightmare suffered by Joe: He is an impotent observer as, "screaming individuals are annihilated." The awfulness of the accident is emphasised by understatement: "the little stick figure flowed or poured across the ground like a drop of viscous fluid."

- Joe analyses his shocked response and is also aware that part of his mind is emotionally detached. He describes Gadd's desperate attempts to pursue his grandson in the balloon in terms of evolutionary psychology: "Such was his genetic investment." Compare this cognitive response with Clarissa's emotional response.

- Joe registers Clarissa's tears as, "no more than a fact." The whole of Joe's reconstruction is emotionally detached. It is fact rather than feeling oriented.

- Joe appears to be fascinated by his own mental and physiological reactions in the immediate aftermath of the accident: "I looked happy, I was wild by now, ready to fight, run, dance." And yet he was aware of a tremor in his legs. What does the way in which Joe ponders every detail of his response convey about his character?

- On page 21 McEwan uses a dramatic metaphor to reveal the significance of Parry in the forthcoming narrative: "the long winter of his obsession."

- Joe describes his behaviour as manic. This is a term used to describe a psychotic state. Thinking of the theme of madness versus sanity in the novel, do you think that Joe, the scientist, could be reflecting upon the nature of mental illness and the boundaries between madness and sanity?

• McEwan's description of Logan's body is shockingly memorable: "Something protruded at the centre of the Þeld, some stumpy antenna of his present or previous self."

• Joe, ever the scientist, describes death as "the closing down of countless interrelated neural and biochemical exchanges combined to suggest to the naked eye the illusion of the extinguished spark." What is the effect of this unusual reßection upon the reader? Does it provoke questions about life and death in your mind? Or does it make you believe that Joe is rather strange in his emotional detachment and scientiÞc curiosity?

• Joe comments upon the upward inßection in Parry's speech and re-members that a linguist explains this modern affectation as a reßection of a world "too mired in relative judgments, too hesitant and apolo-getic to say how things were in the world." Find out about relativism. Why do you think Joe might Þnd the concept of relativism irritating?

• Jed Parry is presented. Examine the language of religious certainty used by Parry. How does Joe react to Jed's insistence? Why?

Chapter 3

Making sense of tragedy: The rationalist cracks...

• Clarissa and Joe sit around the kitchen table examining their perceptions of the afternoon. It is interesting to note that Joe remarks that, "Clarissa told the beginning of her story." He recognises that the way in which people experience the same event is entirely individual.

• Clarissa recalls her perceptions using literary imagery: "Hurled headlong ßaming from the ethereal sky..." Does this poetic way of seeing things aid the accuracy of her perception?

• Joe feels guilt. He shows Clarissa the burn marks on his hands... proof that he had tried to the point of suffering to save the child. Joe's reaction here is emotional rather than rational. Do you think that Joe's emotions cloud his judgment?

• Joe refers to the way each experience their individual consciousness using the metaphor, "we were prisoners in a cell... until our prison grew larger." What is your understanding of subjective experience from this imagery? Is it sharing their perceptions with each other that enlarges the cell? Yet the imagery still insists that our consciousness is a space from which the individual can neither escape, nor exchange for an alternative cell.

• McEwan uses language from the semantic ßeld of construction to illustrate the way in which people build a narrative: "like dedicated craftsmen . . . grinding. . . hammering. . . threading single perceptions into narrative" (p.30).

• Clarissa says that Logan's death "denied the existence of angels." Joe felt that this was 'taken as read.'

• Clarissa ßnds it difßcult to accept that a good man should die in heroic circumstances. Joe, the rationalist, explains her need to make sense of suffering by recounting the story of Clarissa's inability to bear children. "She saw a man prepared to die to prevent the kind of loss she felt herself to have sustained."

• Clarissa said "it must mean something," Joe's response is "I'd never liked this line of thinking." Clearly neither can fully share the perceptions of the other.

•   McEwan describes the psychological effect of love making upon Joe: "It was deliverance." What is the point of this do you think?

•   Clarissa says, "the rationalist cracks at last." She is referring to Joe's manic behaviour after Logan hit the ground. What does she mean by this?

•   Joe and Clarissa have supper with friends and recount their tale "from a place of safety" (p.36). What is meant by this phrase do you think?

•   At the end of this chapter, as Joe and Clarissa lie in bed, Jed phones; he tells Joe "I love you." Joe tells Clarissa that it's a wrong number and admits, "I made my first serious mistake. Being in love implies a shared narrative..." Joe and Clarissa had exchanged perceptions and constructed the narrative of the accident. However, Joe's lie about the phone call keeps her out of his experience with Jed. . . thus allowing cracks to form in their relationship which allow Clarissa to form her own theories about Joe's relationship with Jed.

Chapter 4

Clarissa's brother falls in lust and constructs a new life narrative, and the tale of the comfort seeking dog: illustrating the pitfalls of anecdote and narrative in scientific enquiry...

• Joe reveals that his core ethic as a scientist is the "noble urge to know and understand more."

• The fallibility in the towers of knowledge constructed by scientists is illustrated in the examples of the Hubble telescope and The Titanic (p.39). How do these connect with a central theme in the novel?

• Joe experiences "feelings that he could not identify." These feelings have physical manifestations: "A pricking along my nape and a rawness in my gut..." Why has McEwan included careful detail of Joe's feelings, and how does this connect with central themes?

• The dog story illustrates the temptation to offer subjective analysis of data and to make a 'leap in the dark' by allowing "the power and attraction of narrative to cloud judgment."

• Joe says, "It is not true that without language there is no thought." Joe is challenging the idea that many linguistic experts hold that language constructs thought. Possibly another example of dissent amongst thinkers and scientiÞc experts to illustrate that not all knowledge is secure. Ideas are constructed by one generation of thinkers and scientists, and are often amended or even demolished by a subsequent generation.

• It seems that Joe is unable to have any thought or a feeling without excavating some theory or scientiÞc study: "All day I'd been afraid, wasn't it an elemental emotion, along with disgust, surprise, anger and elation, in Elkman's celebrated cross-cultural study?"

• The question of the origin of Joe's fear appears to trouble him because it seems to be instinctive rather than reasoned: almost a sixth sense! This is very provocative to a scientist dedicated to rational thought: "My fear had held a mask to its face."

• To reinforce this emerging paradox in Joe's character, the end of the chapter shows him returning a jar of ßowers which had been left to mark the spot of the death of a policewoman: "I couldn't help feeling that it might bring me luck a hopeful act of propitiation. On such wild forces whole religions were founded, whole systems of thought unfurled". Almost against his reason Joe Þnds that in moments of stress and anxiety, his mind runs along incomprehensible and irrational lines of superstitious or religious thought. It seems that emotion undermines certainty even for Joe.

• The chapter ends with a cliff-hanger, was Joe being stalked by Jed wearing his trainers with the red laces... or is Joe cracking up?

Chapter 5

The unreliability of feelings

• Joe's thoughts about the reliability of science moves its focus from the 19th century to the 20th century; from narrative in science to examples of the pseudoscientiþc mind. Joe writes about the father of psychoanalysis, Freud, and describes the methodology and scientiþc evidence as "fabulation run riot." However, it is interesting that the very weakness in the work of the 'pseudo scientists' mentioned by Joe is evident in his own work: "It wasn't written in the pursuit of truth, it wasn't science. It was journalism whose ultimate standard was readability."

• Clarissa's brother: "The transmutation of love into indifference." This is an indication of the changing nature of feelings in contrast to the supposed permanence of objective facts.

• Joe acknowledges that his writing is subjective. The examples he used to support his article on the appeal of "aesthetics of form... and elegance in science were fabulously skewed... I was astonished that such puny reasoning, such forced examples, could have held my attention for so long." It seems that Joe's desire to create a cohesive argument had made him selective in the examples he used to support his thesis: the very weakness which he claims undermines the validity of the work of many eminent scientists.

• What do you think is the connection between the anecdote told by Clarissa about her brother's marriage breakdown and the issues about the ways in which knowledge is sometimes garnered? (p.52)

• The chapter closes with Clarissa and Joe making their "nightly journey into sex and sleep." Clarissa's return had "restored Joe completely." Truth and reality for Joe and Clarissa are rooted in their love and commitment to each other.

Chapter 6

Joe's perceptions of Jed clash with Clarissa's perception and Joe meets his stalker...

•   The chapter opens with Joe's continuing analysis of the circumstances that lead to Logan's death. He is tortured by the belief that the death was the responsibility of the rescue group. Joe tries to use his rational mind and his memory to enable him to apportion blame or exonerate himself. Joe's mental reconstruction of the accident typically swings from analytical to emotional mode as he tries to recall who was Þrst to release their grip upon the rope: "Not me! The scales tipping from altruism to self-interest."

•   On page 56 Joe tells Clarissa about Jed's initial phone call. Clarissa is at Þrst amused; she perceives Jed's obsession to be harmless. It is Joe's obvious anxiety that is Clarissa's concern. Her response to Joe's story about the 'laces in the library' is concerned incredulity, "Let me get this straight. You had this idea you were being followed even before you saw his shoe?" Jed is perceived as "a poor fellow with a crush." Do you agree with her perceptions here?

•   Joe's rationality leaves him bereft when Clarissa departs to work: "I felt like a mental patient at the end of visiting hours, don't leave me here with my mind." Why do you think that this phrase Þts so well with a central theme of the novel?

•   Jed's perception of Joe is that he is spiritually needy, and that it is his mission to bring the light of Truth into Joe's life. Jed has no doubts. Joe has hitherto concluded that certainty and truth about anything is elusive, in contrast Jed does not entertain any doubts about the absolute nature of his religion.

•   Joe agrees to meet Jed. He tells himself, "Perhaps I could muster some detached curiosity..."

39248

Chapter 7

Joe meets Jed and there is a clash of 'realities'...

• This chapter focuses upon Jed's declaration of love and his certainty that this love is returned. Thinking of Joe's interest in evolutionary psychology (the belief that our behaviour is programmed to favour the survival of the gene, or more accurately the meme, a current belief held by many scientists and popularised by Richard Dawkins). In what way is this thesis challenged by Jed's love for Joe?

• Jed's perception is that he and Joe are in a relationship. He not only asserts his love for Joe, but is unequivocal in his certainty that his love is returned: "You love me. You love me, and there's nothing I can do but return your love" (p63) .

• Jed believes that "we've come together for a purpose." He is certain that the 'meaning of love' is to bring Joe "to the Christ that is in you and that is you." Clearly this view of the reason for emotions is in sharp contrast to that of evolutionary psychologists.

• Joe's reaction to Jed's religious certainties is surprisingly revealed in an interesting metaphor, "'twas as if I had fallen through a crack in my own existence... what amazed me was how easy it was not to say, 'who the fuck are you? What are you talking about?'" Does a religious, mystical way of thinking come more easily to people than a rational scientibc approach?

• It seems that Jed has presented Joe with an alternative reality, and Joe is, for a split second, confused about what's real, whose perception is true: "it took an act of will to dismiss the sense that I owed this man . . . I was playing along with this domestic drama" (p.67).

• The chapter ends with Jed, in spite of Joe's rejection of his set of beliefs, waving Joe off "forlornly, but looking, without question, like a man blessed in love."

Chapter 8

Theories and subjectivity: "There is nothing either
good or bad but thinking makes it so" Hamlet

• Joe's alarm and distaste for Jed has abated, his feelings have changed; consequently, so has his perception: "Now I considered him to be a confused and eccentric young man, a pathetic Þgure, not a threat at all..."

• Joe writes his article on the baby's smile. How does this Þt in with current evolutionary psychology?

• Clarissa is angry about what she sees as "rationalism gone berserk." Clarissa believes that the theories of evolutionary psychology are "the new fundamentalism . . . everything is being stripped down and in the process some larger meaning is lost." Clarissa contends that "the truth of a baby's smile is in the eye and heart of the parent:" Truth, 'in the eye of the beholder?' How does this relativistic idea Þt with the themes of the novel?

• Joe and Clarissa agree on a compromise perspective that: "there was nothing wrong in analysing the bits, but it was easy to lose sight of the whole . . . the work of synthesis was crucial." However Clarissa says that Joe "still does not understand her:" it seems that Clarissa's perception of love is deeply subjective... and that it is fundamentally at odds with Joe's perception.

• Jed intercepts Joe as he leaves a bookshop. He believes that Joe had told him to wait for him. Joe steps inside the shop and attempts to block Jed's entrance. McEwan writes that Joe saw him "through the unbreakable glass." How might McEwan be using this phrase as a metaphor for consciousness?

• Joe loses his sanguinity... and phones the police. "Being hounded by Parry was aggravating an older dissatisfaction..." Joe begins to long for the clarity and objectivity of science. He acknowledges that what he does is populist science and very much about the manipulation of facts to stimulate his readers. "I can spin a decent narrative... in the science fashion jungle... carrying my own increment to the mountain of human knowledge." How is this last phrase used ironically?

- Joe reßects upon the ßuidity of knowledge, and realises that his own fund of scientiÞc expertise is no longer cutting edge: "I was an outsider to my own profession." Joe realises that his writing is based upon factual information yet it is spun into a narrative; the facts welded together by speculation and conjecture.

- The chapter ends with Jed's message about the curtains. Could this be an allegory used by McEwan to tease the reader? Jed speculates on the movement of curtains and concludes that he knows that Joe is sending him a message. If people are given to delusion when constructing knowledge of any kind, where should we draw the line between subjective interpretation based upon 'cherry picking' facts to Þt with our own ideas, and psychotic delusion? Is madness simply a matter of degree? Why do sane people go mad? Some questions can be answered by medical science and some things are open to speculation and conjecture.

Chapter 9

*Joe attempts third person detachment: he tries
to 'see' from Clarissa's perspective...*

• Joe's attempt at empathy with Clarissa is constructed from hindsight. She has had a bad day and Joe outlines all the circumstances that have combined to produce her feelings/mood when she returns home to Þnd Joe in need of tender loving care. He is seeking to understand the rationale behind her response to his bad day.

• Joe attempts detached self-observation hoping to achieve objectivity: "He is for the moment deaf and blind... hanging in the frame of the door like some newly discovered talking ape..." Meanwhile Clarissa produces her own diagnosis of Jed's state: "a lonely inadequate Jesus freak..." Joe's empathy extends to deÞning Clarissa's thoughts: "they love each other and they happen to be in different mental universes." But is it possible for Joe to inhabit Clarissa's consciousness? Can he really know what she is thinking and feeling?

• Clarissa believes, according to Joe, that "all a theoretical physicist needs besides talent and a good idea is a sheet of paper and a sharp pencil." She also makes a comparison with writing poetry and theoretical physics. What is McEwan getting at do you think? Hasn't he been indicating that there is a gulf between the arts and sciences in the novel in previous chapters?

• Clarissa, according to Joe, begins to think about her father's decline into dementia; it was always "her fear that she would live with some one who goes crazy. That's why she chose rational Joe." Is rationality a defence against mental illness?

• Clarissa makes a mental leap from thinking of her father's delusions to describing Joe's preoccupation with Jed as a 'symptom.' The perceptual gulf between them widens, and Joe tries to understand in retrospect, how it occurred.

• Clarissa rises from the hot bath and feels dizzy and speculates that "something is wrong with her heart." McEwan shows how our thoughts are formed and the irrational narratives that our minds so easily construct.

- Joe and Clarissa move toward judgment of each other and conflict. McEwan anatomises the way in which that conflict arises: "A shift to anger, an accusation, angry words, resentment, and reckless intensifiers. Where do we learn such tricks? Are they inscribed along with our emotional repertoire?"

- Joe tells Clarissa, "there's this problem out there..." but unfortunately Clarissa believes that the problem is within Joe...

- Joe storms out of the flat telling Clarissa, "Well fuck off then!"

Chapter 10

Joe's memory stirs; something he has read:
'The key word was curtain'

• Joe says, "It was Parry of course who was to blame for coming between Clarissa and me." Is this simple statement an accurate summary of the change in the relationship?

• Joe's feelings, evolving out of his row with Clarissa, are the prism through which he begins to indulge the fantasy that: "I was a poor down-and-out scurrying in the rain past rich people's houses. Some people had all the breaks, there was no one out here to care for me now." Joe realises that his mind was being tricked by his feelings: he was deliberately amplifying his self-pity and resentment that he had been so misunderstood. He concludes that "the brain was such a Þne-Þligreed thing that it could not even fake a change in its emotional state without transforming the condition of a million other unfelt circuits." 'We see things not as they are, rather as we are.'

• Jed becomes aggressive, convinced that Joe is taunting him: "giving me all your fucking little secret signals to keep me coming towards you."

• As the extent of Jed's psychotic delusions increase the drama and tension of the scene, Joe thinks that "his condition was so extreme, his framing of reality so distorted that he could harm me." In what way is Joe's reßection about the way in which we frame reality ironic?

• Joe's memory about De Clerambault comes into focus and he returns to Clarissa "with a sudden leap of cheerful love because I was so obviously, incontrovertibly right and she was simply mistaken." What is your reaction to Joe's reappraisil of the difference of opinion between himself and Clarissa?

Chapter 11

The reader 'sees' from Jed's perspective: the psychotic mind?

• Why do you think that McEwan uses the letter device? What is the importance of presenting the relationship between Joe and Jed from Jed's point of view?

• What is the tone of the letter?

• How does the contents of the letter relate to the information given in the appendix?

Chapter 12

Self-delusion: we weave our own truths…

A dictionary definition of science: 'A systematically organised body of knowledge established through observation and experiment'

• The chapter begins with Joe reßecting upon his discontent with his profession, and his unease that he is unable to fathom. McEwan makes reference to 'the talking cure.' This is the name given to Freudian psychoanalysis. Freud was heralded for a time as a great mind: his insights into the human psyche and the origins of psychological disorders were thought to be of great importance to the clinical treatment of these conditions (which was largely to discover the childhood origins of the problem through the patient talking about his childhood and the analyst interpreting them and presenting his conclusions back to the patient). Freud's scientiÞc research was ßawed because his conclusions were based upon work with a narrow group of people; largely middleclass Viennese women. His Þndings were biased because he did not use a representative selection of people. They were all women; they were white, middle class and were presenting with neurotic symptoms. Freud extrapolated from his Þndings, presuming them to be applicable to all people, from both genders, and every background, culture etc. It has also been argued that his theories cannot be tested because any evidence can always be twisted to Þt. In other words his work was unscientiÞc.

• Why do you think that McEwan calls 'the talking cure' a genteel fraud?

• Clarissa reveals that she is harbouring doubts about Joe's state of mind; she has a suspicion that he may have written the letter himself: "His writing is rather like yours..." It seems that in spite of their love for one another and the degree of intimacy between them, Clarissa is unable to really know Joe.

• Joe thinks he knows what Clarissa thinks: "Clarissa considered Parry my fault." Clarissa thinks she knows what Joe is thinking: "I mean the way you're looking at me now, making calculations that I'll never know about. Some inner double entry bookkeeping." However

Joe is actually thinking: "How lovely you are and how I don't deserve you" (p.103). Meanwhile Jed thinks that he knows what Joe is thinking: "You knew our love from the very beginning. You recognised in that glance that passed between us..." (p.93)

• Joe had written a piece on 'self-delusion.' What is the ironic connection between his article and the points above?

• Joe, the clear thinking, rational scientist, is convinced that he knows why Clarissa isn't 'on his side:' "Some hot little bearded fuck-goat of a postgraduate..." What point is McEwan making about facts and the individuals that interpret them?

• The chapter ends with Joe's intended visit to Mrs Logan. His final thought is: "I didn't trust myself." He realises "how dishonestly we can hold things together for ourselves" (p.107).

Chapters 13 and 14

Mrs Logan constructs her own 'truth' from the evidence that her husband had not been alone on the day of the accident...

• Mrs Logan presents Joe with the facts, as she knows them: Her husband's circuitous journey from Oxford to London: "the detritus of a picnic, a chiffon scarf with a lingering scent." From this she constructs a narrative; and it is not tentative. She states, "I know what killed him" (p.122).

• Why has McEwan included Mrs Logan's story? Do you think that it resonates with the themes of the novel? In what way? Some students have argued that it Þts too well, that McEwan labours the point; that the novel is obviously contrived, to the detriment of the book as a whole. What do you think?

• In response to Mrs Logan's torrent of emotion and her conclusion that her husband was "showing off to a girl..." Joe writes "this was a theory, a narrative that only grief, the dementia of pain, could devise." He tells her, "It's so particular, so elaborate. It's just a hypothesis." Mrs Logan has taken facts and through self-delusion has created her own truth, a subjective construction: a personal narrative. Who else in the novel has done this?

• Mrs Logan's children engage Joe in a discussion about cultural practice, moral relativism and absolute truths (p.120). McEwan appears to be referring to truths which are constructed by a society at a particular time and which apply to particular cultures ie. What we can know for a given time. He asks: "Aren't there any rules the whole world can agree on?" for example murder, stealing. These examples are called moral absolutes. How does this apparently incidental chat with the kids echo the central themes in the novel?

• A remark by the boy Leo triggers Joe's memory of the incident of the woman suffering from the delusional illness De Clerambault Syndrome and Joe makes the link with Jed's obsession.

Chapter 15

*Joe makes a journey back to the scene of the accident
and reflects upon the things that have changed...*

• Joe conjectures about the unknown woman with Logan. He is
aware that he is using his imagination. He asks questions and day-
dreams about their possible relationship.

• Joe reßects upon his changed relationship with Clarissa: "I could
not quite imagine a route back into that innocence." What do you think
McEwan is saying here? What has changed and why?

• Joe ruminates upon the nature of love, a central theme in the novel.
Joe thinks about the pathological love epitomised by De Clerambault's
syndrome and says, "For there to be a pathology there had to be a lurk-
ing concept of health." Joe appears to be asking, "what do we mean by
normal? And what is madness?" He refers to the "reckless abandon (of
lovers) to their cause as sanity." Is there a sense in which the 'normal'
condition of being in love involves a distortion of reality; the "dark,
distorting mirror" that Joe says is De Clerambault's syndrome?

• When Joe returns to the ßat, Clarissa is waiting for him. She has
discovered that he has been searching her desk. Her words to him are
oddly reminiscent of Jed's words: "It's a statement, a message, from
you to me, it's a signal. The trouble is, I don't know what it means...
what is it you are trying to tell me?" What do you think that McEwan
is saying about Clarissa's perception?

Chapter 16

Jed's second letter to Joe…

• Jed discovers that much of Joe's scientiÞc writing (for popular journals etc) confronts the Christian fundamentalist view of God and creation. Jed is affronted and passionate in his rebuttal of what he perceives as Joe's dismissal of the Christian religion.

• Jed accuses Joe of "presuming to know so much" in his speculative Bible analysis. Consider Jed's argument: Is it rational? Well constructed? Or does it sound like the ranting of a madman?

• Jed asserts, in response to his reading of one of Joe's articles which offer a neat, godless theory of creation, that: "Describing how the soup is made isn't the same as knowing why it is made, or who the chef is." Is this a reasonable stance do you think?

• Why do you think that McEwan has constructed Jed's careful response to Joe's scientiÞc theories?

• On page 135, Jed says that Joe's "mind is closed" that his "defences are in place." In other words he is accusing Joe of refusing to reßect upon his intellectual stance, and be open to other ways of seeing the world. Can you see the irony in this?

• The chapter closes with Jed's demand that Joe move all his stuff in Jed's place; he writes conÞdently, "You'll probably want to get rid of most of it anyway." What is the irony of Jed's line in the light of his previous accusations of Joe's closed mind?

• The tone of this letter is one of utter conviction, and until the closing paragraph Jed sounds sane, and his theories intellectually reasonable. What is there in his perspective that might be considered unbalanced.

Chapter 17

Clarissa believes that Joe is 'manic, and perversely obsessed' and he realises that he is on his own

• Synaesthesia is the production of a sense impression relating to one sense or part of the body, by simulation of another sense or part of the body. It is a neural experience which is well documented, yet not well understood. Joe says that he is reviewing "Þve books on consciousness." This is a topic currently in vogue with scientiÞc and philosophical thinkers. There are arguments about the deÞnition of consciousness and whether it might be artiÞcially created. Some computer scientists believe that artiÞcial intelligence is a feasible vision of the future, while others believe with equal certainty that a machine will never be truly conscious. Why do you think that McEwan has included these two topics in his novel?

• Joe's self-image is negative in this chapter. He has lost conÞdence in himself as a worthy lover for Clarissa: "muted anger, Þnely disseminated self-loathing, these were my colours." McEwan seems to show through Joe, the changeability of moods and feelings and the way in which our feelings construct our self-perception and shape our view of the world: Should our perceptions then, be trusted?

• On page 143, Joe says that Jed's "world was determined from the inside, he crouched in a cell of his own devising." What is ironic about Joe's metaphorical summary of Jed's (psychotic) view of the world?

• Joe says that Jed "illuminated the world with his feelings," that there is little objective reality in Jed's obsessive relationship with Joe; it is a "prison of self-reference." Joe fantasises about a physical showdown with Jed, although his mind tells him that this is unlikely. Jed predominates in Joe's thoughts and Clarissa is relegated to "the same neural address as Jean Logan's women who believed themselves wronged." Clarissa moves into the spare room telling Joe, "Don't you realise that you've got a problem?" Clarissa becomes progressively more certain that Joe is deluded... and the reader ponders the narrator's reliability.

• Think about the different perceptions of these three protagonists and the validity and errors in each point of view. Which character do you feel most afÞnity with, and why?

Chapter 18

Clarissa thought she could feel her way to the truth…

• Joe assembles the evidence of Jed's obsession. He appears to find taking control of his emotions and behaving logically: the rational way to deal with the situation. Joe reasons that the way to make the police listen to him is to make a complaint. He tells the policeman about de Clerambault's syndrome. The policeman appears to think that it is Joe who may have a psychiatric illness. This is ironic. Explain the policeman's perception.

• Joe says that he "Couldn't quite take (Clarissa's) insistence that we were finished seriously... it seemed the kind of love that would endure." Yet it is Jed's love that the title of the book fits best. How does this fit the themes of the book?

• Joe ponders the idea that there might be "a genetic basis to religious belief." The concept that religious belief might "confer selective advantage" in evolutionary genetics is an objectification of religious belief that is the opposite of Jed's passionate emotional conviction. Would such a genetic basis make religious belief more likely to be accurate in its perceptions?

• At the close of the chapter, Joe theorises about their love making in terms of evolutionary theory. Is he in danger of over-simplification in trying to explain everything with a single theory?

Chapter 19

Science… .Knowledge… Truth…

- Joe and Clarissa arrive at the restaurant to have a birthday lunch with Clarissa's godfather who has "been appointed to an honorary position on the Human Genome Project": Science's quest to know the secrets of life, while Clarissa's gift from her Godfather is a gold double helix. Jocelyn tells an anecdote about the geneticist Miescher (his breakthrough was blocked by his teacher). The progress of knowledge was halted by the chemists who "couldn't see, wouldn't see." Next comes the anecdote about another scientist; Phobus Levine; "He was absolutely certain that DNA was a boring irrelevant molecule... he dismissed it... it became a matter of deep faith with him what he knew, he knew." Is McEwan saying that a sense of *knowing* can be an impediment to reason? That the very feeling that we *know* can be an impediment?

- Joe quotes Keats, "Beauty is truth, truth beauty..." It was also the belief of Albert Einstein that mathematics is beautiful. He said that, "The Theory of Relativity is too beautiful not to be true." Is beauty a good yardstick for judging truth?

- Pontius Pilot asked the profound question which is at the core of this novel, "What is Truth?" Can you attempt an answer to this question?

- After the shooting, Joe says: "It became a temptation to invent or elaborate details about the table next to ours to force memory . . . to deliver what was never captured." Psychology suggests we fill in the gaps and confabulate in order to make our narratives seem to make sense. Is this usually a conscious or unconscious process do you think?

- Clarissa tells the anecdote of "the famous put down." The young Keats visited his hero Wordsworth who delivered "his shocking dismissive put down." Jocelyn asks, "Do we trust the story?" The problem of the fallibility of memory and the difficulty of objectivity seems to turn even the most rigorous academic research into the past lives of those we seek to know, into what Jocelyn describes as "a kind of myth." This prompts the question, 'how much can be known?'

- Joe asserts, "The ßavour of my sorbet was lime." The chapter tells two tales of real life scientists whose work toward the progress of scientiÞc knowledge was diverted or restricted through human fallibility. What is the connection between these anecdotes and Joe's admission that he recognised in himself the temptation to garnish and elaborate facts? The problem of garnering 'unpolluted truth' becomes a difÞcult enterprise when hampered by individual subjectivity in the form of grandiosity and ego-led judgments in the world of Science and of Art. What is it about grandiosity that leads to a resistance to the recognition of new truths? Is this effect at work in any of the protagonists in the novel?

Chapter 20

*Erroneous perception: Our perception consti-
tutes our reality and the truth (as we know it...)*

• Joe attempts to tell the police that he was the intended victim in
the restaurant; however, Wallace, the police inspector, challenges his
perception of the sequence of events, and by implication his belief
that Jed is behind the attempted murder. Joe reßects that, "We could
not agree on anything... we lived in a world of half-shared unreliable
perception, and our sense data came warped by a prism of desire and
belief..." How does the concept of desire and belief as prisms suggest
a link with the anecdotes in the previous chapter? (By analogy with
Newton's use of prisms to split white light into rainbows).

• Joe further reßects that, "Believing is seeing... that metaphysics
and science were such courageous enterprises... set right against the
grain of human nature." McEwan seems to be saying that science and
metaphysics, (abstract ideas about such things as love, being, knowing, identity etc) are both in pursuit of disinterested truth, and yet truth
and knowledge are often elusive because we þnd it difÞcult to ensure
objectivity: Our interpretation of the unalloyed facts is corrupted by
subjective perception ... "There could be no private redemption in objectivity." Is it possible for human beings to ever be truly objective?

• Wallace states with utter conviction: "Parry isn't behind this, believe me." A lack of openness and objectivity is clearly dangerous for
a policeman. Do you know of any real-life crimes that took a long time
to solve as a result of this? Was this because of an inability to maintain
a detatched perspective?

• Johnny Wells, the small time drugs dealer from Joe's past is perceived in his memory as "an honest shopkeeper who kept a simple
heady faith in himself as a philanthropist." Do we believe too readily
in the accuracy of our own recollections or personal value system?

• Joe wryly observes that as "the 1980's got cracking, barristers,
consultants and rock stars concentrated on the money" (the money to
be made indirectly from the drug culture). This is a perception of the
drug industry that has almost been sanitised by perceiving it as simply

a commercial opportunity. Self-interest and self-delusion are further presented as endemic in human relationships.

• It is Joe's belief that "the mind altering substance of choice in a pressured, successful middle life is alcohol." It is the belief of Inspector Wallace that Prozac does the trick. Joe asserts with conviction that damage done by substance abuse is the result of "a defect of character," yet science has recently theorised that the predilection for addiction is genetic.

• Chapter 20 concludes with a cliffhanger as Joe contacts Johnny Wells and tells him, "I need a gun."

Chapter 21

*Contemporary psychologists and philosophers be-
lieve that language constructs thought. In others words
the language that we use constructs our reality, the way
in which we perceive the world and the people in it*

- What is the effect of referring to a gun as "the wherewithal" or "the necessary?"

- The surreal underworld characters in the house are referred to by Johnny as intellectuals. He also says, "They're not too stable..."

- Joe attempts to understand the dog's behaviour by using the kind of narrative which he derided when used by early behavioural psychologists. "It seemed to want to engage me in some form of cross-species complicity, the dog, bereft of the resources of deceit available to me sank back to the earth to await forgiveness."

- Xan declares Joe's stißed laughter masquerading as allergy as "an imbalance; research has shown that in over 70% of cases the roots can be traced back to frustrated needs in early childhood..." Thus popular psychology becomes absorbed into the belief systems of society.

- As Johnny and Joe leave the strange household with the gun, they receive a call from Parry. The chapter ends with a high level of suspense: "I'm at your place with Clarissa..."

Chapter 22

• The denouement in the ßat culminates with the shooting of Parry. The reason that Parry had forced Joe to return to the ßat was not that he intended harm either to Joe or Clarissa; rather that he sought absolution: "If you forgive me, God will too." Parry's religious certainty remains intact. Joe ironically comments, "In a world in which logic was the engine of feeling, this should have been the moment when we moved toward each other... but such logic would have been inhuman." It seems that Joe has reached the conclusion that it is beyond the scope of human endeavour to successfully detach the conscious thought process from the irrational, emotional, subjective response: the inconveniently inaccurate prism through which we perceive the world and the thoughts, feelings and behaviour of people.

Chapter 23

• Chapter 23 is simply Clarissa's letter to Joe. It is conciliatory yet seems to make matters worse between them as it makes their different views more explicit. Under what circumstances does a difference in point of view prove damaging to a relationship?

• In chapter 24 Joe offers new information to Mrs Logan and she is able to construct a completely different narrative from events. She then feels extremely self-critical for wrongly judging her husband guilty of an affair. Is this response reasonable given the apparently compelling but incomplete evidence that she used in making her Þrst judgment?

• Most readers will have shared her initial impression that the evidence is indicative of her husband having had an affair. Is the author trying to say that we can often be wrong even when strong evidence seems to conÞrm our views?

Appendix: de Clerambaults Syndrome

The appendix contains information about the psychiatric condition known as De Clerambault's syndrome. It also contains a case history. The case history is an epilogue about Parry. It is told from the perspective of the clinician dealing with Jed and concludes that he is suffering from the condition known as de Clerambault's syndrome. Joe's diagnosis was correct according to the medical criteria.

The notes conclude that the pathological love that Jed has for Joe continues, and that scientiÞc literature available suggests, "this is indeed a most lasting form of love the pathological extensions of love not only touch upon but overlap with normal experience, and it is not easy to accept that one of our most valued experiences may merge into psychopathology." An Enduring Love!

- What is the effect upon your perceptions of the narrative in the light of the information in the appendix?
- Does it alter the way in which you read the character of Joe?
- Does it alter the way in which you understand the central issues in the novel?
- Do you feel greater sympathy for any of the protagonists in the light of the Þnal disclosures?

Sample Essay 1

*To what extent do you feel that McEwan's use of real
life characters and their work in his novel fits the central themes? Do you believe that the inclusion of these
characters compromises the cohesion of the novel?*

Enduring Love is a novel that can be approached in a variety of
ways, and consequently there is debate over what exactly the novel is
about and how it should be interpreted. It can be viewed, as the critic
Rachel Billington points out, as a fascinating psychological thriller.
McEwan could be presenting the story of Joe, Clarissa and Jed as a
straightforward thriller, with Joe being stalked by Jed. In this analysis
the events are merely an end, they are there purely to fulfill the function of entertaining the reader in what is perceived as aplot-driven
narrative. The critic Nicholas Nesson believes that it is a book about
our responses to violence. There is evidence to support this view; the
novel is concerned with the reaction of people to the violent death of
John Logan. There are also other instances of this, after the gun men
attack the restaurant and Jed holds Clarissa hostage. By taking apart
the various elements in the plot a view such as this is wholly accept-
able. But there is another interpretation that looks beyond the plot to
the overall effect the author is trying to achieve, to the novel's central
theme, that 'unreliability is an ineradicable part of what we are,' according to Adam Mars-Jones.

The novel can then be seen as a philosophical argument that
looks at the ideas that fascinate the post modern world. The ideas
involving the concept of truth are explored in the novel: what is truth?
How can the truth ever be known and can it ever be objective? The
novel can be seen as a book that provides a basis for a philosophical
evaluation of the readers' own beliefs. McEwan achieves this effect
through his use of the three main protagonists and real life characters
that reflect and expand the issues that Joe, Clarissa and Jed face.

In the first chapter of the novel Joe begins to think about Darwin's theory that expressions of human emotion are genetically inscribed. Already the reader is aware of real life characters permeating
the world of these characters. McEwan mentions Darwin in passing,
but he is in the process of setting up the character of Joe. He is watch-
ing people coming out of the arrivals gate at Heathrow and thinks that

this provides proof of Darwin's theory, "I saw the same joy … in the faces of a Nigerian earth mama, a thin-lipped Scottish granny … I kept hearing the same sighing sound on a downward note." McEwan is presenting Joe as a character who searches for answers and reasons, the expressions are purely emotional, but Joe reduces them to biological functions. This is similar to an argument that Joe has with Clarissa over the meaning of a baby's smile, he believes, "That the smile must be hard-wired, and for good evolutionary reasons." Clarissa accepts that analysis of the parts is to be expected but cautions that "it is easy to lose sight of the whole." The way Joe approaches all aspects of his life is with this same analytical eye, as the real life example has shown.

Clarissa is a literary academic and biographer of Keats. Immediately the real life Þgure of Keats is being used to make the reader consider two things. Firstly he can be seen as an arbitrary Þgure because it is the process of creating a biography that illuminates the ideas. Creating a biography is a process that involves collating disputable facts and using them to illustrate a life. The facts are disputable because there has to be a system of selection: what one biographer feels is unimportant another may attach great weight to. These selections then are Þtted together to create a picture which is of the biographer's own making. He or she is making a choice about how the Þgure is presented; a biography is never objective even if it strives to be, because it is coloured by imperfect and emotive human perception. In the same way Clarissa fervently believes that there is a secret lost letter, "It's easy to imagine him writing a letter he never intended to send." Even though she doesn't have this evidence she has imagined the scenario to such an extent that she believes it, and this in turn must affect the way she writes about Keats.

While exploring the ideas associated with biography McEwan chooses Keats for a reason, he too was interested in these ideas. He developed his own ideas about the power of the imagination and how it was at odds with the intellect, he wrote: "I mean Negative Capability, that is when a man is capable of being in uncertainties, Mysteries, doubts, without any irritable reaching after fact and reason." What Keats is trying to get across is that, in relation to his art, pain and pleasure can be represented without a moral judgment being made. Keats is accepting that people live in a state of uncertainty, a world that is irrational where things happen for no reason. McEwan is using this real life character and he Þts the central themes perfectly. It could be said that Clarissa is very much like Keats in the way she approaches events; she accepts that there are things we will never know and moves on from there. On the other hand Jed believes he has the answers and Joe is searching for them. What McEwan is doing in using Keats is presenting the reader with a real life example that says truth is always subjective. Both Keats and Clarissa believe that a strident search for truth is reductive, "…in the process some larger meaning was lost."

McEwan uses real life events as a mirror for the events in the novel. Joe has Þnished writing a piece about the Hubble telescope and has concluded that the telescope was "driven by a simple and noble urge - to know and understand more." But the aims were not fulÞlled because of human error - just as Joe's search for truth and understanding fails as he realises the constraints of perception. He is bound by human nature to be selective in the way he approaches the facts.

Joe has used Darwin's theories to explain the smiles on people's faces. In Chapter Four McEwan shows that Joe's use of 'science' is selective; Joe believes "that Darwin's generation was the last to permit itself the luxury of storytelling." But has this changed? Joe as a science journalist is constantly creating stories from the limited facts he has to hand. He uses a letter published in 1904 about consciousness in animals using the example of a dog: "The writer concluded that the dog must have had a plan," in this case Joe has recognised that telling the story has got in the way of the truth. This real example of a scientist's work exposes a truth about the nature of science: when it is presented human nature changes how it appears; we read things for ourselves, not from others - "…power and attractions of narrative had clouded judgment." Joe talks about the theory set out by Dirac about electrons and light. It was slow to gain acceptance because it did not Þt in with generally held views, "Acceptance withheld on grounds of ugliness." This could be applied to Clarissa's view of Jed; it is easier and more comfortable for her to see him as a harmless eccentric than face the cold reality that he poses a danger. A similar idea is explored when the police can do nothing to help Joe. What Jed is doing doesn't Þt how they see things - it is not accepted because it is 'ugly'. Again McEwan has presented evidence to support a theme in the novel.

Joe is feeling that all his contributions to science have been failures and worthless, he views himself as "parasitic and marginal." His job as a science journalist no longer satisÞes his desires to discover and understand, he feels that he is just taking other people's work and passing it off as his own. These feelings lead him to consider the "talking cure. A genteel fraud;" a reference to Freud's research. At the time of Freud's work he was heralded as a great mind, making huge advances in understanding the human psyche and psychological disorders. Freud's work was used as the basis for clinical treatment of psychological conditions but his research was flawed. Freud was guilty, like Joe, of spinning narratives from very limited evidence. Freud made his conclusions based on very limited evidence from a narrow group of people - middle class Viennese women. Essentially the way Freud approached his research was unscientific and left the results biased - can the whole of humanity be justifiably represented by white, middle class women displaying 'neurotic' symptoms? Freud then expanded what he found here and made it universal, an unscientific assumption and so a "fraud".

Freud is mentioned in the chapter before Joe goes to visit Mrs. Logan. Jean Logan is guilty of much the same thing as Freud, of taking very little evidence and extrapolating a narrative that her husband was having an affair. Like Freud, Jean is looking for an answer and it seems she will inevitably find the one she wants. She cannot accept that the good man she was married to has died, it is more comfortable for her to believe in his affair - the sense of loss is reduced.

An example that is often cited as evidence of McEwan compromising the cohesion of the novel is the birthday lunch in Chapter Nineteen. McEwan spends a large proportion of the time relating anecdotes about DNA and Keats. The meal culminates with Parry's hit men mistakenly shooting at the table next to Joe, Clarissa and Clarissa's godfather Jocelyn, but an intellectual debate is what precedes it. It can be argued that such blatant use of real life characters at this point in the novel slows the plot right down and instead of feeling Joe's panic the reader is faced with a barrage of interesting, but ultimately pointless facts. There is another point of view that these stories are integral to understanding the journey that Joe makes in the novel.

McEwan uses Jocelyn's anecdote about the geneticist Miescher to show how human emotion and self-interest can change 'rational' science. Miescher had speculated "that DNA might code for life" but his superiors "blocked" his discovery, the implication being that self-interest halted scientific discovery. Jocelyn continues with an example of the "chemists ... Very powerful, rather grand." It was people such as these that blocked such a discovery, in this case Phobus Levine. He was certain that DNA was irrelevant, and just as Miescher felt, it was important; "What he knew, he knew, and the molecule was insignificant." What McEwan is doing is stacking up the evidence to show how futile Joe's quest for the truth about the accident is - it is human nature to protect oneself. Joe has acknowledged this: that they jumped from the balloon, "The scales tipping, from altruism to self-interest." Just as their actions at the time were molded by human nature so will be their accounts of the events.

In this same chapter there is Clarissa's account of a meeting between Keats and Wordworth. Jocelyn asks "But do we trust this story?" From Clarissa's negative answer it would seem that it is historically unreliable to accept it as fact, it exposes the fallibility of memory and problems associated with objectivity. Interestingly though, "... the story lives on ... A kind of myth." The academic study of a person's life has been reduced to conjecture and "myth." Jocelyn puts forward the idea that the account continues to be prevalent because "we need it." How is it that such unreliable anecdotes are accepted so widely and are deemed necessary by an intelligent man? What it does is fuel the human instinct for story telling, the stories that enable us to understand events - "It isn't true, but it tells the truth." Here are two different interpretations of what truth is: can the story be accepted because it represents the men's subjective construing of the facts and evidence? Another example used is that of God, many people come to understand Him through the scriptures, which are stories.

McEwan uses numerous real life characters and stories in his work to provide substance to the philosophical arguments his characters are having. Clarissa, when writing her Keats biography recognises how important this is: "she needed more evidence, different sources." McEwan recognises that if his novel is to function as a philosophical argument there has to be real life propping up his fictional characters' viewpoints. But the use of these real life individuals can compromise the cohesion of the novel, with the plot getting lost among the various scientists, writers and thinkers. To what extent this damages the novel's cohesion depends on how the book is viewed. It is important to recognise that it is "a novel of rich diversity" (Peter Kemp) and as such perhaps fails to fulfill every readers' expectations. As a psychological thriller these real life figures serve as minor distraction from the events of the novel. However by including these figures McEwan is inviting the reader to explore post-modern ideas with him and so in this sense their inclusion gives the novel its strength. There are instances, such as Clarissa's birthday lunch, where the flow of the narrative is interrupted to the detriment of the scene but when looked at in its wider context the discussion on DNA is hugely inßuential for both the characters and the readers understanding.

McEwan has created an exciting thriller while making sure that none of the intellectual ideas he wants to examine are left unexplored. I believe that he has succeeded in creating a thought-provoking novel which succeeds in making the fallibility of human perception and rationality clear to any reader. What lesson could be more worthwhile than to realise than how easily we all make fools of ourselves?

Sample Essay 2

The three central protagonists in Enduring Love could be said to represent Science, Art and Religion. In the light of this statement, how far does this account for the conflict between the characters?

Love that endures is a main theme in the novel, and the strongest force in existence, which has the capability of bridging the gulf of perception between those whose outlooks are diametrically opposite, for example, Art, Science and Religion (Clarissa, Parry and Jed). However, this only bridges them, it does not resolve any differences they may have in terms of perspective. I do not think it is possible to answer the above question without touching on why these three topics are diametrically opposed. I intend to answer this as well as to explore the characters' differences, and whether these spring from their individual opposing outlooks.

Paradoxically, the characteristics of art, science and religion that cause them to be diametrically opposed are discreet, yet at the same time obvious. The character of Joe represents science within the novel. Through the novel, we learn how Joe lives up to his scientiÞc outlook on life and there is ample evidence of him being very empirical. This is displayed in the very Þrst chapter, "Later I wondered why it had not been blown away. Later still I discovered that the wind at Þve hundred feet was not the same that day as the wind at ground level."

Because of his scientiÞc characteristics, he believes that everything must be based on fact. He has an overriding need to establish facts in order to see his truths and believes only in rational actions, particularly in human beings. Further evidence of this is the revisiting of the accident repeatedly in his mind, and the eventual physical revisiting to the scene of the accident, in chapter Þfteen, to Þnd answers.

However, this theory, along with many of the ideas and opions asserted by Joe, is ßawed. In trying to understand the chain reaction that occurs within the novel, he himself acts irrationally and with genuine feeling, but of course, does not recognise what he previously referred to as irrational when he experiences these feelings himself. For example, in the very Þrst chapter when Joe meets Clarissa from the airport: "…in thirty-Þve minutes I experienced more than Þfty theatrical happy endings, each one with the appearance of being slightly less well acted than the one before… and suspected that even the children were being insincere. I was just wondering how convincing I myself could be in greeting Clarissa... immediately my detachment vanished, and I called out her name with all the rest."

He analyses the behaviour of the people at the airport and criticises its genuineness until his "detachment vanishes" and he experiences it himself. As the novel progresses, we learn that this involuntary hypocrisy is typical of Joe. He observes people as if they were playing out a drama; an interpreted world through narratives: a Þction. However, this is very interesting, as each of the character's own truths are based around this idea of a Þctional narrative. For Clarissa, she is a university English literature teacher, Joe is a scientiÞc journalist, and Jed suffers from a delusion. Therefore, the conßict, which arises between the characters because of their contrasting truths, is ironic. The previous quote is just one an example of Joe contradicting his beliefs. Evidence of this increases as the novel progresses.

The scene at the airport is also an example of a much more implicit contradiction on the part of Joe; "If one ever wanted proof of Darwin's contention that many expressions of emotion in humans are... genetically inscribed, then a few minutes at Heathrow's terminal four should sufÞce." Yet later, he questions the sincerity of these actions, which would suggest Darwin's theory is not accurate. In addition to this, there is the differing statement he makes in reference to the accident. At Þrst, his view is; "A child alone and needing help. It was my duty to hang on, and I thought we would all do the same." A contradiction he believes simultaneously is that, although he did not know who let go Þrst; he is certain it was not him. However, just a few pages on from this, he states: "The child was not my child, and I was not going to die for it." This contradiction proves his irrationality where strong feelings are involved, yet he does not recognise this in himself as he does in other people. This idea is carried through the novel to the extent that it is almost a central theme and I wonder, although it does not state anywhere, if this is the McEwan's authorial voice shining through, subtly showing he does not believe in Joe's outlook.

I also assume that McEwan aims to highlight the weaknesses in Joe's beliefs, perhaps to say that even the dedicated rationalist is a prisoner of the irrationality that is inherent in human kind.

The character of Clarissa, representing art within the novel, is very different from Joe, just as Art is very different from Science. Her outlook on life is diametrically opposite to Joe's. One very clear example of this is the debate on a baby's smile in chapter 8, where "human nature was up for re-examination..." Joe cannot accept simple answers as Clarissa is able to. Joe's belief is the same as that of Edward O. Wilson; "...it is a social releaser, an inborn and relatively invariant signal that mediates a basic social relationship." Clarissa on the other hand believes, "the truth of the smile is in the eye and heart of the parent, and in the unfolding love which only had meaning through time." At this stage in the novel, Clarissa and Joe's enduring love bridges their differences: "there we left it, no hard feelings." As the novel progresses, theses two completely different perspectives are exposed further. The introduction of Parry into their lives exposes their diametric opposed viewpoints, resulting in a growing conßict between the two characters. Evidence for this increasing tension lies in chapter nine, where Joe and Clarissa move towards judgment of each other after an argument about Jed. The ripple effects of the balloon accident at the start of the novel, is the main cause of the crack which has occurred between them, and the beginning of the problems in their relationship. Further into the novel, Clarissa becomes progressively more certain that Joe is suffering from a delusion, not Jed, and as a result, a less severe conßict grows between the reader and Joe as we question his reliability as a narrator. What I found extraordinary in the novel, is that once we see the breakdown of trust between Clarissa and Joe, we as readers feel a breakdown of trust between Joe and ourselves: "His handwriting is rather like yours" (page 100) suggests Clarissa's disbelief in Joe's story. Our breakdown of trust is a direct result of Joe's unreliable narratives, which signify a turning point in the novel, as our opinions of Joe alter and we see him in a more negative light. As an unreliable narrator, we understand, through the thought provoking themes, that everything he says cannot be relied on, as the facts are tainted; an altered truth.

The third protagonist, Jed, represents faith and religion in the novel. Jed is a young, gay male suffering from de Clerambault's Syndrome, as we Þnd out towards the end of the novel. From our very Þrst encounter with Jed, we as readers come to our own conclusions about his behaviour. "What we can do is pray together." This is not the sort of behaviour considered normal outside of religious groups, and his religious zeal feels uncomfortable. Straight away, we label his unnatural fervor as mad because it seems irrational and inappropriate to most people. However, once you analyse the other central characters, evidence suggests they too are, or go through, stages of being mad according to the same criterion. Joe shows this with his manic behaviour, both after the accident and towards the end of the book when he travels to get the gun. This behaviour is noticeable by others, "the rationalist cracks at last" (Clarissa), which later form into accusations that Joe is the mad one, but this is never noticed by the character themselves. This is also similar to Clarissa's situation, after circumstances left her unable to bear children: "I had never witnessed such a disabling grief..." (Joe) This resulted in her decline into depression after the death of her friend's baby. To an extent, her experiences have rendered her incapable of rationality in some circumstances: "... Clarissa's own mourning for a phantom child..." The idea that all the characters experience some kind of madness is likely to be a comment by McEwan about society. In terms of the story, it seems ironic as each of them believe their own construing of the world and that their beliefs are the truth, yet can any of them be relied upon if they all see *reality* as 'they are:' That is through a prism of unreliable subjectivity? I think McEwan is asking, "Is this a universal truth for all of us, that there is no such thing as a reliable human narrative?"

Because of our questioning the reliability of the narrator, I found myself questioning on a number of occasions, who out of Jed and Joe was actually the mad one? Although at the beginning of the novel we are presented with this religious extremist, with an absolutist idea of God, it is all from Joe's perspective, until we read Joe's letter, which has not been tainted by a secondary perspective. The letters, in which he writes, appear so plausible and rational: "Describing how the soup is made is not the same as describing why it is made..." As a result, we are left with the question of the reliability of Joe as a narrator, and we question the reliability of Joe's perspective of the conflict between the two characters.

Science is based on reality, truth, facts and rational thought. You do not simply believe and see or see to believe; in the scientific method there is the obligation to predict and then objectively test a scientific model. Art is 'the creation of something beautiful or significant' (dictionary). Therefore, although art is often an expression, it uses a human interpretation to create a reality; you see to believe in many cases. Religion is dissimilar to both of these. Religion is based more upon faith than hard-headed evidence, it does not rely on the correctness of the success of its predictive model (answered prayer?) and is therefore much less tangible. Any actual event may be interpreted as being due to the greater wisdom, or capriciousness of an omniscient God. Believing is seeing in this case. Each belief system contradicts the others and it is therefore understandable how three people with these differing contexts for construing perception could come into sharp conflict with one another.

Linking in with this idea, in chapter nineteen we meet Clarissa's Godfather. He mentions past eminences in the field of science who "… could not, or would not see the truth of the scientific evidence before them because the evidence conflicted with their pet theories." This idea is relevant to each character but alters to fit their characters. To Keats, the imaginative mind was diametrically opposed to the intellect. It was capable of "being in uncertainties, mysteries, doubts without any irritable reaching after fact and reason." It is therefore easy to understand that three different perceptions: Art, Science and Religion can explain the conflict between the characters.

The main conflict that develops between Joe and Clarissa is the debate on the reoccurring events surrounding Jed Parry's obsession, which is rooted in the breakdown of trust between the two characters.

At the end of the novel, the future in the relationship between them is left open. Clarissa writes in a letter to Joe, "I was completely wrong… but there might have been a less frightening outcome if you had behaved differently…you were manic, and driven, and very lonely." This lack of trust, which creates a fracture in their relationship, is, a result of the characters being blinded by their own 'truths', which results in a lack of empathy and understanding between them. This happens to those who claim to know the truth; This rather arrogant perspective is common in people and to all the characters in the novel, including those not central to the story, Mrs. Logan for example.

Mrs. Logan constructs her own truths, based on the facts of the day of the balloon accident. "I know what killed him." As this happens to each of the characters, it is likely to be a comment made by McEwan in reference to society and how we all construct our own narratives based on our own perceptions which are unreliable but taken as fact. It is therefore inevitable that conflict arises, as each person's view of the world is different, and each is convinced of their own rightness. I believe all these ideas are a huge insight into McEwan's ideas. Being so confident that your theory is correct, can blind you and result in mistrust with other theories and people, just as it does in the novel. This mistrust can be destructive; we see in Mrs. Logan the effects her husband's death has had when she believes he had an affair: "Her sourness…anger in her voice…" and later reference to a scarf which she believes the "mistress of my husband" owns.

Therefore, to sum up what I think McEwan is trying to say, is that being blinded by your views, and having the inability to escape from a tunnel vision mind, which is often self-constructed, can be destructive, yet we are all culpable of this psychological trick in everyday life. A lesson from reading the book is "to hold beliefs lightly and to be open to new evidence." A reader who reaches this conclusion will have gained an invaluable beneßt from his or her encounter with the novel.

The conßict between science and religion (Jed and Joe) is also a big theme. The behavioural scientist, Noakes, writes, "A rationalist scientißc mind is set up in opposition between the values of the heart and the domestic scene." What is interesting about the two characters representing science and religion is that we often question Joe's sanity, as his truths are ßawed, even though it is Parry who is mad in a more clinical sense. I do not believe that it is an accident that their names are so similar, nor do I think it a coincidence that there are more similarities between the characters when we look further into the iceberg. They both proclaim to know truths, we doubt Jed because of his illness, but Clarissa, who is supposedly sane, doubts Joe, and therefore so do we. Our opinion of one character is highly inßuenced by another. Could this be another comment on society by McEwan? Is he arguing that once a person is labeled mad by someone, we see them in that light and consider them so ourselves, constructing our own little stories on the situation. Noakes also states that: "Truth is a ßctional narrative," and this could be a ßve word summary of the central theme of the novel.

Sample Essay 3

The three central protagonists in Enduring Love could be said to represent the conflicting truths of Science, Art and Religion. In the light of this statement how far does this count for the conflict between the characters Joe, Jed and Clarissa.

D.H. Lawrence once wrote, "If it be not true for me, what care I what truth it be." Insinuating perhaps that we as human beings construct our own truths, and instead of there being absolute truths there are rather relative truths. These ideas have exercised academic minds and are aspects of relativism that underpin post-modern philosophical ideas. McEwan presents these ideas in the novel, when he writes that, "believing is seeing," meaning that we see selectively, and what we do see is inßuenced by the beliefs that we hold. The three central protagonists in Enduring Love are representative of the conßicting truths of Science, Art, and Religion. The conßict between the central characters in the novel is arguably the fact that they all have fundamentally different beliefs and their truths: what they each know for sure, is different. To what extent could this conßict between the characters be attributed to their differences in beliefs?

Joe Rose is the narrator in Enduring Love and is also representative of Science in the novel. His use of language reveals this, in that many of the expressions he uses to describe events are scientiÞc, "…comforting geometry… mathematical grace." These two terms are based on mathematical imagery; mathematics is an objective truth, one that we can all know for sure. This helps give insight into the character that McEwan presents, and it seems that Joe's profession, as a scientiÞc writer, inßuences the way in which he describes his narrative, and his perceptions of events.

A deÞnition of science is, "…a systematically organised body of knowledge established through observation and experiment." Joe Rose seems to believe that he can get at truth through a rational and systematic way of thinking. This is evident in Joe's attempt at describing his love for Clarissa. In the love letters he writes; he says that: "all that sincerity would permit me were the facts." Joe's attempts at deÞning his love through facts conveys to the reader the way in which Joe explores even his own feelings through logical and factual reasoning. It also serves to demonstrate Joe's emotional detachment, which is also evident in his description of John Logan's death: "…the closing down of countless interrelated neural and biochemical exchanges."

"Faith, being belief that isn't based on evidence, is the principal vice of any religion," so says Richard Dawkins an eminent scientist, and like Joe an atheist. Joe defines his truth using rational thinking and a scientific approach. The existence of God cannot be scientifically proven, so he has no confidence in religion, as he has no evidence. Joe is impressed with the arguments of Charles Lyell: "The earth was a lot older than the four thousand years defended by the church." It seems that Joe uses Science to help substantiate his claim that there isn't a God. Interestingly Jed Parry uses science to help substantiate his claim that there is a God: "...the more we learn about the intricacies of God's creation, the more we realise how little we know." This is a point of conflict for the two characters in the novel as they each have fundamentally different beliefs. It also causes the reader to question how so called objective truths as presented by Science and Mathematics, can be interpreted so differently.

The novel as a whole is punctuated by real life case studies in which the interpretation of factual information is flawed. The reader is informed that Miescher's findings on DNA are blocked by his teacher who, "couldn't see, wouldn't see." It is shown that even when provided with scientific evidence and the truth, (as we now all perceive it), the teacher still maintained the belief that DNA was irrelevant. It is stated in the novel that it became a matter of faith with him, his absolute: what he knew for sure. This demonstrates the fact that people's beliefs influence what they hold to be true.

Clarissa is representative of Art and works as a biographer. She is researching Keats and pieces together information about his life to present an absolute truth. However every biographer has a different opinion and a different truth. Clarissa has no evidence of Keats writing a letter to his love Fanny Brawne before he died; yet she believes that in the same situation she would have written a letter. "It's easy to imagine him writing a letter he never intended to send."

It becomes evident in Chapter one that Joe and Clarissa are very different. It seems that while Joe is emotionally detached, and attempts to construct and describe his truths using objective opinions, Clarissa's truths are subjective, in that they are influenced by her personal feelings and understanding. Clarissa uses literary imagery to describe her experiences. "...Hurl'd headlong flaming from th' Ethereal Sky," whereas Joe describes his experiences through scientific imagery. His description of John Logan's body shows this: "...at the moment of impact the little stick figure flowed...like a drop of viscous fluid." This shows that the manner in which each character's perception and description of events is influenced by their beliefs; Clarissa speaks in terms of literary imagery and Joe uses scientific imagery.

Keats was a romantic poet, and was opposed to the manner in which science reduces everything to facts. As Keats's biographer Clarissa would be aware of the concept of negative capability, described by Keats, as being capable "...of being in uncertainties, mysteries, doubts, without any irritable reaching after fact and reason." (Keats's letter) Clarissa is representative of metaphysical ideas in the book: abstract ideas like love, being, knowing and identity. This is a point of conflict for Joe and Clarissa in the novel. As Joe is described as being driven by the desire to "know and understand more," he is unable to be in uncertainty and applies reason and logic in his pursuit of truth. This contributes to the conflict between the characters.

Jed parry is a fundamentalist Christian; his speeches in chapter two reflect this, as there are many religious references, for example to God and prayer. Jed believes that it is his mission to bring Joe to God, "... To bring you to God, through love."

It is interesting to note that each of the main character's views on the nature of love are widely different. Clarissa views love as a metaphysical absolute, in that it is beyond physics, it is an abstract idea and cannot be defined through rational thought. It is seen that Clarissa is opposed to the way in which Joe attempts to reason it away through science. This is evident in Clarissa's reaction to Joe's thoughts on the nature of a baby's smile. Evolutionary psychologists believe that a baby's smile is: "...a social releaser, an inborn and relatively invariant sign that mediates a basic social relationship" (p70).

In other words, it is an innate characteristic designed to ensure a baby's survival; this is the thesis of Richard Dawkins book, 'The Selfish Gene.' Clarissa views this way of thinking as reductionism, and asserts that: "Everything was being stripped down... in the process some larger meaning was lost." It can be seen that the concept of negative capability is evident here. Clarissa is opposed to the manner in which Joe attempts to define love through facts and reasoning. Clarissa declares that: "...The truth of that smile was in the eye and heart of the parent and in the unfolding love which only had meaning through time." Joe however is unable to truly comprehend what Clarissa means and admonishes that he too, is talking about love and "how babies who could not yet talk got more of it for themselves." It seems that each of the characters mentioned are unable to fully share each other's perceptions regarding the nature of love and their ideas are influenced by the core beliefs that they hold. It is shown here that the views held by the two characters contribute to the conflict in their relationship, as they are each unable to understand each other's views.

Jed Parry presents another view on what the nature of love is. Jed views love as a way to bring Joe to God. Joe Rose is challenged by this idea; if, as evolutionary psychologist believe, love is a biological trick to ensure procreation then Jed's love for Joe defies evolutionary theory. Why would a man love another man? There can be no survival value in an emotional and sexual relationship between individulas of the same sex. Joe attempts to rationalise Jed's argument: "…you keep using the word love. Are we talking about sex?"

The manner in which each of the central characters try to define the nature of love, shows that their perceptions are very much based on the beliefs that they hold. Clarissa's beliefs about love reflect the metaphysical ideas held by the Arts. Joe attempts to apply rational thinking and science, to describe the nature of love; and Jed is influenced by religion in his interpretation of what love is, viewing it as means by which we can grow closer to God: "My love- which is also God's love- is your fate." It could be argued that Jed's insistence that he shares God's love for Joe is his way of coming to terms with what is regarded as abhorrent behaviour by religious fundamentalists. This is a point of conflict between the characters that can be attributed to their fundamental differences in belief, their beliefs arc shown to influence what they hold to be true and the characters of Joe and Clarissa appear to be challenged by their differences in beliefs. "Consolation is harder for science to provide." (Richard Dawkins), and perhaps this is what first triggers the conflict between Joe and Clarissa. The two characters have different needs; Clarissa needs to know John Logan died for a reason, "Logan's fall was a challenge no angel could resist, and his death denied their existence," (Clarissa) Joe's response is: "Did it need denying?" His response is a point of conflict for the two characters as it is a question which challenges Clarissa's ability, like Keats's, to embrace the mystery. This point is further substantiated in chapter eight when Clarissa asserts: "…You've got us trapped in our genes, and there's a reason for everything!" It seems that whilst Joe can derive comfort from facts and rational thoughts as demonstrated by his reference to the "comforting geometry," in chapter one, Clarissa cannot, as it challenges the idea of negative capability.

The conflict between Science and Religion can be dated back to the 14th Century, when Cecco d'Ascoli, was burned by the Church for daring to suggest that men might live on the opposite side of the globe. The conflict between science and religion continues today, the major conflict being the consensus in modern science of the mind being a physical machine and that the soul doesn't exist. Joe presents these ideas in the novel: "…why a pre - scientific age would have needed to invent the soul."

Much of the conflict between the characters, Joe and Jed, arises from the conflict in their beliefs. On Joe's initial meeting with Jed, Joe asserts: "…But I decided he ought to know the truth. Because, my friend, no one's listening." Joe's truth is that there is no God, and his truth conflicts with Parry's version of the truth. Jed is affronted by the way that Joe attempts to explain away religion using science. Jed refers to Joe's ideas using the metaphor of "dirty washing," emphasising Jed's disgust for the views held by Joe. Jed writes: "…do you think faith could depend on a length of rotting cloth?" This is interesting as it demonstrates that Jed is utterly convinced that his truth is the 'real' truth, and even when it is contradicted by scientific evidence, his convictions remain the same and he is not challenged in the same way that Joe is.

Arguably Jed is not challenged at all by Joe's beliefs as he is so adamant that he is correct, whereas Joe does feel challenged: "…It was as if I had fallen through a crack in my own existence, down into another life." Here everything that Joe perceives, and his way of looking at the world is being challenged. Could Jed's inability to reflect and revise his world-view be an aspect of his madness?

It could be argued that not all of the conflict between the characters could be attributed to the conflict between Science, Art, and Religion. After the balloon incident, Joe and Clarissa thread, "single perceptions into narrative," in other words they construct their version of the truth together. After the conversation between Joe and Parry, Joe fails to tell Clarissa about it, and therefore leaves her to form her own truth about Jed Parry, instead of having a joint truth. This contributes to the conflict in their relationship, and Joe admits that it was his "…first serious mistake." Later Joe decides that it is Parry who is driving a gulf in their relationship: "…it was Parry of course who was to blame for coming between Clarissa and me." This perhaps contributes to the conflict between Joe and Jed.

There is a limited amount of conflict between the characters Clarissa and Jed and perhaps this could reßect the fact that there is less conßict between the Arts and Religion. The two characters' beliefs therefore are relatively similar, both Parry and Clarissa embrace the mysteries in life: "…There are mysteries too we should not touch" (Jed).

Much conßict can be seen to arise from the character's differences in beliefs, mainly because each character believes that they possess the real truth, and they attempt to convert the other characters to their way of thinking by challenging them on the beliefs. Jed writes in his letter that: "…you'll have to explain yourself to all of your friends, not only your change of address, but the revolution in your beliefs."

Joe writes that: "metaphysics and science were such courageous enterprises…set right against the grain of human nature… disinterested truth," implying perhaps that to hold absolute truths like those held by the three central protagonists, is brave, as those beliefs are constantly being challenged by other people. The quote could also be interpreted as McEwan commenting on the nature of truth and how objectivity is hard to ensure, and does not come naturally to human beings. Science is based on fact, it is when these facts are interpreted by people that problems arise, as the facts are then subject to a person's perception. McEwan conveys this idea, of how truth is very rarely pure through the use of the unreliable narrator, Joe Rose, who describes his sorbet in vivid detail in one chapter and in the very next chapter, he contradicts himself. Joe asserts in chapter nineteen that: "…the ßavour of my sorbet was lime, just to the green side of white," later he says the ßavour of his sorbet was apple. This causes the reader to be unsure of what the actual truth is, and so the reader questions the absolutes being portrayed by the narrator, and questions whose truth is correct. There are also points in the novel where Joe acts irrationally. It seems that Joe's emotions compromise his ability to think rationally. "What was stopping her from being on my side? Some hot little fuck-goat of a post-graduate…" This is effective in demonstrating how McEwan presents Joe as an unreliable narrator, and also shows how disinterested truths are very hard to achieve.

McEwan's presentation of Jed's letters also cause the reader to question the narrator, the argument he presents in the letter is very rational and does not appear to reßect Joe's perception of Jed as insane.

It is seen that the major conßict between the characters is due to their differences in perceptions. It has been demonstrated that the characters fundamental beliefs are inßuential in the way they perceive events. I conclude that it is really the conßict between the differing ways of construing meaning that are inherent in Science, Art, and Religion that contributes to the majority of the conßict between the characters.

39248